EMILY IN PARIS

The French are Ringarde!
Romantics but
they're also La Plou
Realists emily
bonjour in
It's like PARIS
wearing I feel like
poetry I'm dreaming
and I'm about
You're in Paris now to wake up
SEXY OR SEXIST?!

THE OFFICIAL

EMILY IN PARIS

COCKTAIL BOOK

VIRGINIA MILLER

weldon**owen**

Contents

French Aperitifs

French Herbal & Bitter Liqueurs

French Mocktails

Introduction

Paris has captivated the world for centuries. Whether due to the romance of the Belle Époque or the freedom of 1930s cabaret culture, the City of Light and Love has inspired endless stories of both finding oneself and finding love—with fabulous food, drink, and fashion as the backdrop, of course. The lineage of stories about Americans in Paris is likewise rich, including *An American in Paris, Breathless, Sabrina, Sex and the City*, and, now, *Emily in Paris*.

Emily—with her winning entourage of friends (Mindy, Camille, and Gabriel) and coworkers (Sylvie, Luc, and Julien)—is a Chicago transplant with a passion for luxury fashion but who has much to learn about Parisian style and cultural differences. Cocktails are an American creation, yet, obviously, the love of good drink is universal. And aperitif hour—*l'heure de l'apéro*, a time

for lingering predinner or late afternoon over a carefully crafted cocktail—is one of France's great cultural rituals.

The history of spirits in France goes back hundreds of years and has brought us some of the world's finest liquors. French brandies alone, such as Cognac, Armagnac, and Calvados, are among the globe's most respected distilled beverages. French herbal liqueurs, like the well-known Chartreuse but also génépy (or génépi), Bénédictine, and such beautifully bitter liqueurs as Suze and Salers, are beloved by drink geeks everywhere. Then there is the ultimate French herbal spirit, absinthe, and its siblings, pastis, Herbsaint, and anisette.

Modern-day France, like much of the world, is experiencing a craft-distilling and cocktail renaissance, with French gins, whiskys, and other spirits being produced around the country. Likewise, for a decade plus, Parisian cocktail bars, such as Little Red Door and Le Syndicat,

have rocked The World's 50 Best Bars list and other drink-industry rolls. But drinking culture has been inherent to the soul of Paris for centuries, whether a pastis with water at a sidewalk café, Champagne for all occasions, or incomparable French wines with dinner.

The recipes in the following pages celebrate Parisian drinking culture, both historical and contemporary, *Emily in Paris*–style, with verve, playfulness, and a to bridge cultural gaps. In chapter 1, Modern French Cocktails, combinations featuring some of France's prized craft gins, vodkas, whiskys, and other spirits, as well as modern-day French cocktails, are explored. In chapter 2, The Green Fairy, French anise-centric spirits, including absinthe, Herbsaint, pastis, and anisette, turn up in such cocktail-hour favorites as the Jet Pilot and Death in the Afternoon. Chapters showcasing French brandies (Cognac, Armagnac, Calvados, and eaux-de-vie), French aperitifs (vermouth,

Champagne, and wine), and French herbal and bitter liqueurs (Chartreuse, génépy, Suze, and Salers) follow. Nonalcoholic cocktails—aka mocktails—are trending the world over and are more well-crafted than ever. The final chapter showcases a range of libations that call for the same mixology rigor as cocktails but use only zero-proof ingredients.

In these pages you'll discover the well-known and the forgotten, the newest creations and century-old favorites, signature drinks and riffs on classics, refreshing spritzes for summer and spirited for winter. As always, quality spirits and other ingredients make all the difference in the taste integrity of any drink, so take the opportunity to seek out small-batch spirits, including the intriguing new ones coming out of France.

Now begin your journey through the deep wealth of French spirits, cocktails, and *joie de vivre* with Emily and friends via the streets of Paris. *À votre santé!*

Modern French Cocktails

GIN

TEQUILA

VODKA

WHISKY

Citadelle Melon Fizz

Since their launch in 1996, the Citadelle gins of Maison Ferrand
have become among France's most popular gins. Citadelle Jardin
d'Été, released in 2021, is inspired by Citadelle founder Alexandre
Gabriel's wife, Debbie Gabriel, and her lush French garden. The spirit
is bright with melon, lemon, yuzu zest, orange peel, even Sichuan
pepper—twenty-two botanicals in all. Although Citadelle Jardin d'Été
features Charentais melon, a French cantaloupe variety, any flavorful
cantaloupe or honeydew melon will play off the fleshy melon notes of
the base spirit. With a touch of sparkling wine, it's a fizzy beauty: an
all-day sipper ideal on a Parisian spring or summer day.

1 oz (30 ml) Citadelle
Jardin d'Été gin

1 oz (30 ml) cucumber
juice (page 123)

1 oz (30 ml) melon juice
(page 123)

¼ oz (7.5 ml) simple syrup (1:1)

1 oz (30 ml) dry sparkling
wine, chilled

Cucumber strip and melon
ball for garnish (optional)

Makes 1 cocktail

COUPE GLASS

Combine the gin, cucumber juice,
melon juice, and simple syrup
in a shaker. Add ice and shake
vigorously until well chilled,
20–30 seconds. Strain into a
chilled coupe glass and top with the
sparkling wine. If desired, garnish
with the cucumber strip and melon
ball on a pick.

Mauresque

The Mauresque (French for "Moorish"), which dates to the early 1800s, was originally made with absinthe but has evolved into a signature French pastis cocktail, particularly in Marseille, where it has been the city's emblematic aperitif since the 1930s. The drink's purity turns milky white as the anise liqueur begins blending with the water. Sip this Marseille tipple at sunset with a snack of olives or nuts, and you'll be transported to the ancient port city.

1½ oz (45 ml) absinthe or pastis
¾ oz (20 ml) orgeat
About 4 oz (120 ml) water, chilled
Star anise pod for garnish

Makes 1 cocktail
COLLINS GLASS

Pour the absinthe and orgeat into a collins or highball glass. Stir gently, then add ice. Top with the water. Garnish with the star anise pod.

LIBATION NOTE

For a gin-forward variation, reduce the absinthe or pastis to ¼ oz (7.5 ml) and add 1½ oz (45 ml) gin, ½ oz (15 ml) fresh lemon juice, and ¼ oz (7.5 ml) orgeat.

French Dry Martini

The roots of the martini are the stuff of legend, with strong arguments on its mid-1800s creation. One common theory is that bartending legend "Professor" Jerry Thomas created it at the Occidental Hotel in San Francisco for a gold rusher on his way to nearby Martinez, California. Another popular story is that it was concocted in San Francisco but was inspired by the classic Martinez cocktail from the town of the same name. Later theories suggest it originated at New York's Knickerbocker Hotel in 1906. Regardless, a cold gin martini remains one of the greatest and most gratifying cocktails of all time, especially when pouring quality gin and vermouth.

2 oz (60 ml) French gin, such as Citadelle or G'Vine

1 oz (30 ml) French dry vermouth

Green cocktail olives or lemon twist for garnish

Makes 1 cocktail

NICK AND NORA OR COUPE GLASS

Combine the gin and vermouth in a mixing glass filled with ice and stir until well chilled, 20–30 seconds. Strain into a chilled Nick and Nora or coupe glass. Garnish with the olives on a pick or the lemon twist.

LIBATION NOTE

If you prefer a vodka martini, substitute French vodka (a well-known brand like Grey Goose or CÎROC or the fair trade–certified quinoa-based FAIR vodka) for the gin. If you prefer a rounder versus drier martini, reduce the dry vermouth to ½ oz (15 ml) and add ½ oz (15 ml) less-dry blanc vermouth.

Dirty Margarita

Even if this riff on the margarita isn't for everyone, salt seekers and dirty martini lovers will take to it immediately. A classic margarita's already happy companionship with salt goes even brinier in this version created in the early 2010s by Rob McHardy at the Paris members-only nightclub Silencio, opened by film director David Lynch. This love child between the dirty martini and the margarita gains its saltiness from caper juice.

1½ oz (45 ml) blanco tequila

½ oz (15 ml) fresh lime juice

½ oz (15 ml) Cointreau or other orange liqueur

¼ oz (7.5 ml) caper juice

¼ oz (7.5 ml) agave syrup

Freshly grated lime zest for garnish

Makes 1 cocktail

COUPE OR COCKTAIL GLASS

Combine the tequila, lime juice, Cointreau, caper juice, and agave syrup in a shaker. Add ice and shake vigorously until well chilled, 20–30 seconds. Strain into a chilled coupe or cocktail glass. Garnish with a dusting of the lime zest.

Bobby Burns

The Bobby Burns is a variation on the Scotch whisky classic Rob Roy cocktail but veers French with a touch of Bénédictine. The exact origin of the Bobby Burns, like that of many great cocktails, is unclear. Even the name, which most believe is an homage to Scottish poet Robert Burns, is disputed. Earliest iterations of the drink in print date to 1902. The *Savoy Cocktail Book* version calls for Bénédictine, and a book from the Waldorf–Astoria adds ½ barspoon absinthe. The Bénédictine version highlights the chocolate and dark fruit notes in the Scotch, while the absinthe version leans lighter and brighter. Either way you drink it, it's a boozy late-night sip.

2 oz (60 ml) blended Scotch whisky

1 oz (30 ml) sweet vermouth

2 dashes Angostura or other aromatic bitters

1 barspoon Bénédictine, or ½ barspoon absinthe

2 maraschino cherries for garnish

Makes 1 cocktail

COUPE GLASS

Combine the whisky, vermouth, bitters, and Bénédictine in a mixing glass filled with ice and stir until well chilled, 20–30 seconds. Strain into a chilled coupe glass. Garnish with the cherries on a pick.

LIBATION NOTE

For a more pronounced French accent—and a lighter, softer version—use elegant Brenne Ten, a 10-year-old single-malt whisky made by a French company with a female founder, Allison Patel.

Au Revoir Savoir

Inspired by the cocktail first published by pioneer Charles H. Baker, this drink is based on the tequila classic, Mexican Firing Squad, which Baker discovered at La Cucaracha Cocktail Club in Mexico City. There are varying strong opinions on how many dashes of bitters to add. The more Angostura bitters, the greater the layers of fall-like spices, so add to your taste preference. Here, the Mexican classic is married with the French 75 (page 74) to become the Au Revoir Savoir, making it an all-day drink.

2 oz (60 ml) blanco tequila

¾ oz (20 ml) fresh lime juice

¾ oz (20 ml) grenadine

4–5 dashes Angostura bitters

2 oz (60 ml) Champagne or dry sparkling wine

Lime twist for garnish

Makes 1 cocktail

CHAMPAGNE FLUTE

Combine the tequila, lime juice, grenadine, and bitters in a shaker. Add ice and shake vigorously until well chilled, 20–30 seconds. Strain into a chilled champagne flute and top with the Champagne. Garnish with the lime twist.

LIBATION NOTE

Prefer the more intense original Mexican Firing Squad? Switch to a rocks glass, omit the Champagne, serve over ice, and garnish with a lime wheel.

Camille, the French Blonde

Purportedly around since the 1920s, the French Blonde is a deceptively breezy mélange of vodka, grapefruit juice, Lillet Blanc, and a floral hit from elderflower liqueur, the right kind of tribute to Emily's fun-loving blonde—and French—friend, Camille. If you prefer to add herbaceous layers, substitute a London dry or herb-forward gin for the vodka and grapefruit-rosemary bitters for the lemon bitters, then garnish with a sprig of rosemary.

2 oz (60 ml) Lillet Blanc

1 oz (30 ml) vodka

½ oz (15 ml) elderflower liqueur

2 oz (60 ml) fresh grapefruit juice

1 barspoon fresh lemon juice

2–3 dashes lemon bitters

Thyme sprig and
grapefruit slice for garnish

Makes 1 cocktail

COUPE GLASS

Combine all the ingredients in a shaker. Add ice and shake vigorously until well chilled, 20–30 seconds. Strain into a chilled coupe glass. Garnish with thyme sprig and grapefruit slice.

"Paris seems like a big city, but it's really just a small town."

—CAMILLE

Chinese Popstar

Emily's best pal, Mindy Chen, left Shanghai in embarrassment after her botched audition for *Chinese Popstar*, a televised singing competition. As she gets her singing confidence back in the streets and cabarets of Paris, we celebrate her gorgeous voice with this cheeky twist on the Porn Star Martini, a modern-day cocktail created by London bartender Douglas Ankrah at The Townhouse bar in Knightsbridge in 2002. Despite the name, Ankrah's sweet-tart combo of vanilla and passion fruit bears no resemblance to the original gin martini. Here, the addition of lychee—in honor of Mindy—results in a sweeter, creamier cocktail, while the finish of Champagne delivers a dry backbone.

2 oz (60 ml) vanilla vodka, such as CÎROC

1½ oz (45 ml) high-quality lychee fruit purée, such as The Perfect Purée of Napa Valley brand

½ oz (15 ml) fresh lime juice

½ oz (15 ml) simple syrup (1:1)

2 oz (60 ml) Champagne or dry sparkling wine, chilled

1 fresh lychee, peeled, for garnish

Makes 1 cocktail

COUPE GLASS

Combine the vodka, lychee fruit purée, lime juice, and simple syrup in a shaker. Add ice and shake vigorously until well chilled, 20–30 seconds. Strain into a chilled coupe glass and top with the Champagne. To garnish, working from the bottom, slit the lychee two-thirds through, then, using the slit, rest the fruit firmly on the glass rim. Alternatively, spear the seeded fruit on a pick.

The Green Fairy

ABSINTHE

HERBSAINT

PASTIS

ANISETTE

Absinthe Suissesse

Invented in New Orleans in the 1890s, this Big Easy staple—and brunch favorite—is one of the city's great classic cocktails that many nonresidents still don't know about, but should. Its generous absinthe and Herbsaint base makes it an ideal Parisian drink, even though "Suissesse" is a nod to Switzerland's historic role in absinthe production. This creamy, nutty, minty beauty is boozy and playful, as sublime for dessert as it is a cool soother on a hot summer day.

1 oz (30 ml) absinthe

½ oz (15 ml) Herbsaint

¾ oz (20 ml) heavy cream

½ oz (15 ml) orgeat

¼ oz (7.5 ml) white crème de menthe

1 egg white

Fresh mint sprig for garnish

Makes 1 cocktail

ROCKS GLASS

Combine the absinthe, Herbsaint, cream, orgeat, crème de menthe, and egg white in a shaker and dry-shake for 30–60 seconds to emulsify and aerate the mixture. Add ice and shake vigorously until well chilled, 20–30 seconds. Strain into a rocks glass over tightly packed crushed ice. Garnish with the mint.

Death in the Afternoon

Ernest Hemingway's 1932 novel *Death in the Afternoon* includes brooding musings on Spanish bullfights and mortality, thoughts appropriately accompanied by a bracing hit of absinthe and Champagne. While the proportions of the cocktail of the same name vary depending on which version you use, Hemingway's directions—recorded in the 1935 book *So Red the Nose or Breath in the Afternoon*—are dangerous: "Pour 1 jigger of absinthe into a Champagne glass. Add iced Champagne until it attains the proper opalescent milkiness. Drink 3 to 5 of these slowly." Three to five of these could do anyone in, but one is an exhilarating delight that feels oh-so-Parisian. If you live for anise, go lighter on the Champagne; if you prefer a bit more effervescence, go heavier.

½ oz (15 ml) absinthe

Simple syrup (1:1) (optional)

2–3 oz (60–90 ml) Champagne or dry sparkling wine, chilled

Makes 1 cocktail

CHAMPAGNE FLUTE

Pour the absinthe into a champagne flute. If a touch of sweetness is desired, add a few drops of simple syrup. Slowly top with the Champagne.

"You came to gray Paris and brought out the sunshine for all of us."

—GABRIEL

Corpse Reviver No. 2

Corpse Revivers, a family of cocktails with little in common aside from their potency, were originally regarded as hangover cures bold enough to "revive a corpse." Their earliest mention in print was in the mid-1800s. A century later, Harry Craddock included recipes for both Corpse Reviver No. 1 and Corpse Reviver No. 2 in his widely distributed *The Savoy Cocktail Book*, published in 1930. In the recipe for the latter, which proved the more popular drink, Craddock called for Kina Lillet, which was made with the bitter agent quinine, unlike the quinine-free current-day Lillet. By the way, the jury is still out on whether the cocktail actually brings back the dead.

¾ oz (20 ml) gin

¾ oz (20 ml) fresh lemon juice

¾ oz (20 ml) Cocchi Americano

¾ oz (20 ml) orange curaçao or other orange liqueur

2 dashes absinthe

Makes 1 cocktail

COUPE GLASS

Combine all the ingredients in a shaker. Add ice and shake vigorously until well chilled, 20–30 seconds. Strain into a chilled coupe glass.

LIBATION NOTE

Cocchi Americano, an Italian aperitif wine with a moscato base, herbs, citrus peel, cinchona bark (the original source of quinine), and other botanicals, comes close to bringing a touch of Kina Lillet's quinine bitterness to the cocktail. You might also try Tempus Fugit's richer, robust Kina L'Avion d'Or, made from a Cortese grape base infused with wormwood, citrus, cinchona bark, and other exotic seasonings. If you prefer sweeter with no bitterness, use Lillet Blanc.

Absinthe Frappé

Bartender Cayetano Ferrer invented the absinthe frappé in 1874 at what would become New Orleans's legendary Old Absinthe House, which still serves the quick-and-easy neon-green cocktail today. Reportedly a favorite drink of Mark Twain and Oscar Wilde, it was a popular morning cocktail until the United States banned the sale of absinthe in 1912. Herbsaint and Pernod were the typical stand-ins for absinthe in the following decades, but once the ban was lifted in 2007, absinthe classics saw new life, including this cooling high-proof frappé.

6–8 fresh mint leaves

1½ oz (45 ml) absinthe

½ oz (15 ml) simple syrup (1:1)

2 oz (60 ml) soda water

Fresh mint sprig for garnish

Makes 1 cocktail

DOUBLE ROCKS OR FOOTED
HIGHBALL GLASS

Muddle the mint leaves in a shaker to release their oils and aromatics, then pour in the absinthe and simple syrup. Add ice and shake vigorously until well chilled, 10–20 seconds. Strain into a double rocks or footed highball glass filled with crushed ice. Top with the soda water. Garnish with the mint sprig.

LIBATION NOTE

A squeeze of lemon or lime, rind and juice, will perk up the frappé with an acidic kick. Ferrer's original version included a couple drops of anisette, powering up the anise profile a bit.

Jet Pilot

This absinthe-tinged tiki-bar favorite is a high-octane good time. It showcases three unique rums, which are crucial to the drink's bold layers of flavor. Spicy cinnamon and nutty Falernum notes play nicely with tart citrus and the anise of absinthe. Donn Beach, one of the founding fathers of tiki-bar culture, created the Test Pilot in Los Angeles around 1941, naming it for an important moment in US aviation history. The quaffable, complex drink inspired many riffs, with the most famous being the Jet Pilot, invented by actor and restaurateur Stephen Crane at his Beverly Hills bar, Luau, in 1958. Crane's addition of cinnamon syrup while subbing grapefruit juice for the Test Pilot's original curaçao amps up the spice and citrus.

1 oz (30 ml) overproof Jamaican rum

¾ oz (20 ml) overproof Demerara or aged rum

¾ oz (20 ml) gold rum

½ oz (15 ml) fresh lime juice

½ oz (15 ml) fresh grapefruit juice

½ oz (15 ml) Falernum

¼ oz (7.5 ml) cinnamon syrup

4–6 dashes absinthe

1 dash Angostura or other aromatic bitters

Fresh mint sprig and Luxardo maraschino cherry for garnish

Makes 1 cocktail

HURRICANE OR DOUBLE ROCKS GLASS

In a blender, combine the rums, lime juice, grapefruit juice, Falernum, cinnamon syrup, absinthe, and bitters. Add ½–1 cup ice and blend on high speed until blended, 10–15 seconds. Pour into a hurricane or double rocks glass. Garnish with the mint and the maraschino cherry.

LIBATION NOTE

If you want a spirituous sipper, this Jet Age cocktail also tastes beautiful shaken rather than blended and served over crushed ice.

Mindy's Morning Glory Fizz

The Morning Glory Fizz is an ideal brunch cocktail because it feels so current. But it was created in the late 1800s as a hair-of-the-dog hangover cure, purportedly by bartender Harry Johnson, and appeared around the same time in two cocktail books: O. H. Byron's *The Modern Bartenders' Guide* and George Winter's *How to Mix Drinks*. Although bracing with Scotch and absinthe, silky egg white, bright citrus, and refreshing club soda make it easy to drink at any time of the day. Emily's bestie, Mindy, reflects the sunny yet complex spirit of this crowd-pleasing cocktail.

2 oz (60 ml) whisky (preferably blended Scotch)

½ oz (15 ml) fresh lemon juice

½ oz (15 ml) fresh lime juice

½ oz (15 ml) simple syrup (1:1)

1 egg white

2–4 dashes absinthe

1–2 oz (30–60 ml) club soda

Orange slice or twist for garnish

Makes 1 cocktail

HIGHBALL GLASS

Combine the whisky, lemon juice, lime juice, simple syrup, egg white, and absinthe in a shaker and dry-shake for 30–60 seconds to emulsify and aerate the mixture. Add ice and shake vigorously until well chilled and frothy, about 30 seconds. Strain into a highball glass filled with ice and top with the club soda. Garnish with the orange slice.

Brunelle

Found in the 1935 edition of *Old Mr. Boston De Luxe Official Bartender's Guide*, this simple ode to the Green Fairy is one of the greatest and most underrated absinthe cocktails of all time. While historically the lemon juice and absinthe ratios are close, tweaked versions over the years allow for a more refreshing, balanced tipple by amping up the lemon.

2 oz (60 ml) fresh lemon juice
½ oz (15 ml) absinthe
½ oz (15 ml) simple syrup (1:1)

Makes 1 cocktail

NICK AND NORA GLASS

Combine all the ingredients in a shaker. Add ice and shake vigorously until well chilled, 20–30 seconds. Strain into a chilled Nick and Nora glass.

Remember the Maine

In his famed book *The Gentleman's Companion*, world traveler Charles H. Baker claims to have discovered the Remember the Maine in Havana during the Cuban Revolution of 1933. Manhattan fans will appreciate the classic drink's whiskey and sweet vermouth lushness, while Sazerac lovers will relish the touch of absinthe. Cherry Heering (the original recipe in Baker's book calls for cherry brandy) adds woody, nutty cherry notes that make this a nighttime imbibement: chic, classic, and boozy.

¼ oz (7.5 ml) absinthe for rinsing

2 oz (60 ml) rye whiskey

¾ oz (20 ml) sweet vermouth

⅓ oz (10 ml) Cherry Heering

Luxardo maraschino cherry for garnish

Makes 1 cocktail

COUPE OR COCKTAIL GLASS

Rinse a chilled coupe or cocktail glass with the absinthe and pour out the excess. Combine the whiskey, vermouth, and Cherry Heering in a mixing glass filled with ice and stir until well chilled, 20–30 seconds. Strain into the absinthe-rinsed glass. Garnish with the maraschino cherry.

Cocktail à la Louisiane

Also known as De La Louisiane or La Louisiane, this heady cocktail was the house drink at the historic New Orleans restaurant La Louisiane in the 1880s, though five decades would pass before it first appeared in print, in Stanley Clisby Arthur's 1937 *Famous New Orleans Drinks and How to Mix 'Em*. Taking inspiration from New Orleans's great Vieux Carré cocktail, this variation skips the Cognac and adds a few dashes of absinthe, upping the drink's herbal whispers. The original calls for equal parts of rye whiskey, sweet vermouth, and Bénédictine, but the Bénédictine has been dialed down here to balance out the sweetness and let the whiskey and vermouth shine (it also makes it slightly lighter proof than its boozier Vieux Carré or Sazerac cousins).

1 oz (30 ml) rye whiskey

1 oz (30 ml) sweet vermouth

½ oz (15 ml) Bénédictine

3 dashes absinthe

3 dashes Peychaud's bitters

2 Luxardo maraschino cherries for garnish

Makes 1 cocktail

COUPE OR COCKTAIL GLASS

Combine the whiskey, vermouth, Bénédictine, absinthe, and bitters in a mixing glass filled with ice and stir until well chilled, 20–30 seconds. Strain into a coupe or cocktail glass. Garnish with the cherries.

Alfie's Tuxedo No. 2

Brought back to prominence at bars like the now-shuttered Douglas Room in San Francisco, the more-than-a-century-old Tuxedo No. 2 was a classic worth reviving. A spirituous gin-and-vermouth sipper layered with maraschino liqueur, orange bitters, and an absinthe rinse, it was version two of the original Tuxedo cocktail. The earliest written Tuxedo recipe is found in Harry Johnson's *Bartenders' Manual*, circa 1900. Old Tom gin was originally used—and makes a lovely version— but using slightly drier London dry gin and blanc vermouth instead of dry vermouth allows the sweet-nutty touches of maraschino liqueur and anise to shine. We may not have had the pleasure of seeing Alfie in a tuxedo, but he's worn the hell out of every suit, thus making this cocktail just the right tribute to Emily's English boyfriend.

¼ oz (7.5 ml) absinthe for rinsing

2 oz (60 ml) London dry gin

¾ oz (20 ml) blanc vermouth

¼ oz (7.5 ml) maraschino liqueur

4 dashes orange bitters

Orange twist and Luxardo maraschino cherry for garnish

Makes 1 cocktail

NICK AND NORA OR COCKTAIL GLASS

Rinse a chilled Nick and Nora or cocktail glass with the absinthe and pour out the excess. Combine the gin, vermouth, maraschino liqueur, and bitters in a mixing glass filled with ice and stir until well chilled, 20–30 seconds. Strain into the absinthe-rinsed glass. Garnish with the orange twist and cherry.

French Brandy

COGNAC

ARMAGNAC

EAUX-DE-VIE

CALVADOS

Brandy Sazerac

The Sazerac is the official cocktail of Louisiana and one of New Orleans's greatest drinks. As with nearly any classic cocktail, its exact origin is debated, but a commonly accepted story is that it was created by Antoine Peychaud in his French Quarter apothecary in 1838 and featured his favorite French brandy, Sazerac de Forge & Fils Cognac. In 1873, New Orleans bartender Leon Lamothe reportedly added a dash of absinthe to the popular drink. By the late nineteenth century, phylloxera had killed off countless vineyards in France, making Cognac difficult to get in the States, so bartenders swapped in American rye whiskey. But this spirit switch is also debated, as old newspaper clippings list rye in the Sazerac at NOLA's original Sazerac Bar. Longtime New Orleans bartender and drink historian Chris McMillian (currently owner of Revel Cafe & Bar) makes the case for the Sazerac's whiskey roots, while Cognac brands argue otherwise. Both versions are good, but a Cognac version feels appropriately French.

¼ oz (7.5 ml) absinthe for rinsing

1¾ oz (50 ml) Cognac

½ oz (15 ml) simple syrup (1:1)

3 dashes Peychaud's bitters

Lemon peel for garnish

Makes 1 cocktail
ROCKS GLASS

Rinse a rocks glass with the absinthe and pour out the excess. Add 1 large ice cube to the glass. Combine the Cognac, simple syrup, and bitters in a mixing glass filled with ice and stir until well chilled, 20–30 seconds. Strain over the ice cube into the rocks glass. Garnish with the lemon peel.

LIBATION NOTE

For a still-French middle ground between bracing grain-based American rye whiskey and elegant, grape-based Cognac, make the Sazerac with the often more robust French brandy Armagnac.

Brandy Crusta

Created by Italian bartender Joseph Santini in New Orleans in the mid-nineteenth century, the brandy crusta was a NOLA staple for decades. The first known printed recipe appeared in *The Bar-Tender's Guide* by Jerry Thomas, published in 1862, alongside recipes for gin and whiskey versions. The drink has experienced a renaissance in recent years, thanks to bartenders like Chris Hannah of New Orleans's lauded Jewel of the South restaurant and bar, who revived it during his fourteen years at Arnaud's French 75 bar.

Sugar and lemon wedge for rimming, plus 1 lemon

2 oz (60 ml) brandy

½ oz (15 ml) orange curaçao

½ oz (15 ml) fresh lemon juice

½ oz (15 ml) simple syrup (1:1)

2 dashes Angostura or other aromatic bitters

Makes 1 cocktail

WINEGLASS OR COUPE GLASS

LIBATION NOTE

Today, many versions of the brandy crusta call for maraschino liqueur instead of simple syrup to add nutty cherry notes. If you like, coat only half of the glass rim with sugar so extra sweetness is an option with each sip.

Pour a modest mound of sugar onto a small, flat plate. Rub the lemon wedge along the outer rim of a chilled wineglass or coupe glass. Tip the glass so it is almost parallel to the plate and roll its lemon-dampened edge in the sugar to create a sugar rim, being careful not to get any sugar on the inside of the glass. Using a vegetable peeler or channel knife, and beginning at one end of the whole lemon, cut the zest from the lemon in a continuous wide strip, then coil the strip and carefully slide it into the sugar-rimmed glass. It will uncoil and spiral up the sides of the glass.

Combine the brandy, curaçao, lemon juice, simple syrup, and bitters in a shaker. Add ice and shake vigorously until chilled, 10–15 seconds. Strain into the prepared glass.

Jack Rose

With both New York and New Jersey claiming to be its birthplace, the roughly 125-year-old spirit-forward but fruity Jack Rose was likely originally made with apple brandy from New Jersey's Laird & Company, the oldest licensed distillery in the United States. The drink remained popular throughout Prohibition, was reportedly a favorite of John Steinbeck's, and merited a mention in a Hemingway novel (*The Sun Also Rises*). While American apple brandy, or applejack (the "Jack" of Jack Rose), was the original base spirit of this drink, elegant French Calvados seamlessly ushers it into Parisian life. A high-quality grenadine—the source of the cocktail's lovely rosy hue—will make all the difference. It also tastes amazing made with lime in place of lemon.

1½ oz (45 ml) Calvados or apple brandy
¾ oz (15 ml) fresh lemon juice
½ oz (20 ml) grenadine
Lemon twist for garnish

Makes 1 cocktail
COUPE GLASS

Combine the Calvados, lemon juice, and grenadine in a shaker. Add ice and shake vigorously until well chilled, 20–30 seconds. Strain into a chilled coupe glass. Garnish with the lemon twist.

Vieux Carré

New Orleans is famed for creating many of history's most legendary cocktails, and the Vieux Carré (meaning "old square"), named after the city's iconic French Quarter, is one of the greatest. It was invented in the 1930s by Walter Bergeron when he was bartending at NOLA's historic Carousel Bar (then called the Swan Room) in the Hotel Monteleone. This drink feels like a meeting between the United States (rye whiskey, bitters) and France (Cognac, Bénédictine). It's boozy, sweet, spiced, and layered, making it ideal for sipping on a romantic Paris night.

¾ oz (20 ml) rye whiskey

¾ oz (20 ml) Cognac

¾ oz (20 ml) sweet vermouth

1 barspoon Bénédictine liqueur

2 dashes Peychaud's bitters

2 dashes Angostura bitters

Maraschino cherry and/or lemon twist for garnish

Makes 1 cocktail
ROCKS GLASS

Combine the whiskey, Cognac, vermouth, Bénédictine, and both bitters in a mixing glass filled with ice and stir until well chilled, 30–40 seconds. Strain into a rocks glass over 1 large ice cube. Garnish with the cherry and/or lemon twist.

"I just don't know what to do with all this happiness."

—SYLVIE

Serendipity

This modern-day classic from the Bar Hemingway in the Ritz Paris was created by its longtime bartender, Colin Field. The story goes that on New Year's Eve of 1994, Field served the just-invented drink to well-known businessman and bar regular Jean-Louis Constanza, and Constanza, on tasting it, exclaimed "Serendipity!" In addition to Paris, the cocktail nods to Normandy with its Calvados (apple brandy) base amped up with apple juice. Quality apple juice is of utmost importance here: Use juice that's directly from an apple orchard or farm, or unfiltered, fresh-pressed, and with no sugar added. Thanks to the Champagne and mint, this is a drink that works any time of the day and into the evening.

3 fresh mint sprigs

1½ oz (45 ml) Calvados or apple brandy

1½ oz (45 ml) unfiltered apple juice

1 barspoon simple syrup (1:1)

2–3 oz (60–90 ml) Champagne

Makes 1 cocktail

HIGHBALL GLASS

Combine 2 of the mint sprigs, the Calvados, apple juice, and simple syrup in a highball glass. Gently muddle and stir. Fill the glass with ice, then top with the Champagne and stir gently and briefly. Garnish with the remaining mint sprig.

Sidecar

The origin of the Sidecar, as with so many classic cocktails, is hotly debated. But one prominent theory puts its creation at the Ritz Paris in the Roaring Twenties. Back then it was an equal-parts drink as shown in *Harry's ABC of Mixing Cocktails* by Harry MacElhone and *Cocktails: How to Mix Them* by Robert Vermeire, both published in the early 1920s. Subsequent editions of the books show the Sidecar moving away from that cloyingly sweet original to more like what you see here.

Sugar and lemon wedge for rimming

2 oz (60 ml) brandy, such as Cognac or Armagnac

¾ oz (20 ml) orange liqueur

¾ oz (20 ml) fresh lemon juice

Makes 1 cocktail

COUPE OR COCKTAIL GLASS

Pour a modest mound of sugar onto a small, flat plate. Rub the lemon wedge along the outer rim of a chilled coupe or cocktail glass. Tip the glass so it is almost parallel to the plate and roll its lemon-dampened edge in the sugar to create a sugar rim, being careful not to get any sugar on the inside of the glass.

Combine the brandy, orange liqueur, and lemon juice in a shaker. Add ice and shake vigorously until well chilled, 20–30 seconds. Strain into the prepared glass.

> **LIBATION NOTE**
>
> For a slightly less sweet but still visually attractive drink, rim only half the glass to allow for sips with and without sugar.

Champs-Élysées

Named after Paris's most famous avenue, the Champs-Élysées cocktail showcases two oh-so-French spirits: Cognac and green Chartreuse. Some recipes call for yellow Chartreuse, and both versions are worthwhile. But green Chartreuse is used in the first recipe in print from Nina Toye and A. H. Adair's *Drinks—Long and Short* (1925). With its 1920s elegance, this herbaceous sipper is an ideal evening choice.

1½ oz (45 ml) Cognac

¾ oz (15 ml) fresh lemon juice

½ oz (15 ml) simple syrup (1:1)

¼ oz (7.5 ml) green Chartreuse

2 dashes Angostura bitters

Lemon twist for garnish

Makes 1 cocktail

COUPE GLASS

Combine the Cognac, lemon juice, simple syrup, Chartreuse, and bitters in a shaker. Add ice and shake vigorously until well chilled, 20–30 seconds. Strain into a chilled coupe glass. Garnish with the lemon twist.

Moulin Rouge Metropole

Opened in 1910, the Hotel Metropole on New York City's West Forty-Third Street was known for its sketchy clientele of gamblers, bookies, actors, and cabaret performers until it went bankrupt only two years later, following the shocking murder of a gambling-den owner just outside its door. Named for the hotel, the Metropole cocktail is essentially a nineteenth-century Cognac martini with a dry, bracing profile. Its connection to the notorious hotel links perfectly to the racy history of Paris's Moulin Rouge as the birthplace of the can-can. And if this potent drink doesn't make you want to join a line of high-kicking dancers, you can instead snap selfies like Emily and Mindy did outside the Moulin Rouge before drunkenly deleting the @emilyinparis Instagram account.

1½ oz (45 ml) Cognac

1½ oz (45 ml) dry vermouth

2 dashes Peychaud's or other Creole-style bitters

1 dash orange bitters

2 maraschino cherries for garnish

Makes 1 cocktail

COCKTAIL OR NICK AND NORA GLASS

Combine the Cognac, vermouth, and both bitters in a mixing glass filled with ice and stir until well chilled, 20–30 seconds. Strain into a chilled cocktail glass or Nick and Nora glass. Garnish with the cherries on a pick.

Café Brûlot

Café brûlot is the ultimate brunch coffee cocktail, a flaming showstopper first served at New Orleans's Antoine's restaurant in the 1880s. The invigorating coffee-and-brandy drink was inspired by French pirate Jean Lafitte, who would make drinks streetside to distract onlookers while his crew picked their pockets. In New Orleans, café brûlot continues to be served tableside for dessert and at jazz brunches in a dramatic display. First, a clove-studded citrus peel spiral is held above a silver bowl of flaming Cognac while ladlefuls of the spirit are poured over it, setting it afire. Then the flaming peel is dropped into the bowl and steaming-hot coffee is slowly poured into the bowl, dousing the fire. In the 1990s, legendary bartender Dale DeGroff got New Yorkers hooked on this Big Easy classic at the Rainbow Room in Rockefeller Center.

Peel of 1 orange, cut into strips 1 inch (2.5 cm) long by ⅛ inch (3 mm) wide

Peel of 1 lemon, cut into strips 1 inch (2.5 cm) long by ⅛ inch (3 mm) wide

6 whole cloves

3 sugar cubes

1 cinnamon stick, 2 inches (5 cm) long

1 cup (240 ml) Cognac

½ cup (120 ml) orange curaçao or other orange liqueur

2 cups (480 ml) hot, freshly brewed black coffee

Makes 4–6 cocktails

COFFEE MUG OR DEMITASSE CUP

Unless you are trained in the complex and exciting flaming citrus peel presentation described above, the easiest way to make this cocktail is on the stove top. Stud 6 of the citrus peel strips with the cloves. In a saucepan, combine all the citrus peel strips, the sugar cubes, and cinnamon stick and set over low heat. Slowly pour in the Cognac, orange liqueur, and coffee until the sugar is dissolved. Ladle into coffee mugs or demitasse cups and serve hot.

LIBATION NOTE

Switch to a deep cherry flavor profile by substituting a cherry brandy, such as Kirschwasser, for the orange liqueur.

French Aperitifs

VERMOUTH

CHAMPAGNE

WINE

Champère Champagne Julep

While you don't have to spray yourself with Champagne, as Emily's Champère marketing campaign urges, you can celebrate Champère-style with Champagne cocktails. Juleps date to the 1700s in the American South, where the cool, minty, crushed-ice beauties in striking silver cups were ideal for the steamy days common in the region. But it's part of the julep's tendency to veer well beyond bourbon. Brandy, rum, and Champagne juleps all have a long lineage. Combining French brandy (whether Cognac or Armagnac) and Champagne is the ultimate French imbibement, though Champagne alone is still a gloriously easy drink—and a lower-proof sipper at that.

8–10 fresh mint leaves

½ oz (15 ml) Cognac, Armagnac, or other brandy (optional)

¼ oz (7.5 ml) rich simple syrup (2:1)

1 dash Angostura or other aromatic bitters

3 oz (90 ml) Champagne or dry sparkling wine, chilled

Mint sprig and lemon slice for garnish

Makes 1 cocktail

JULEP CUP OR ROCKS GLASS

Gently muddle the mint leaves in a julep cup or rocks glass to release their oils and aromatics. Combine the Cognac (if using), simple syrup, and bitters in a shaker. Add ice and shake vigorously until well chilled, 10–20 seconds. Fill the julep cup roughly three-fourths full with crushed ice, then strain the shaker contents over the ice. Slowly add the Champagne and stir briefly to mix but not to dilute. Add more crushed ice to form a dome above the cup rim, then garnish with the mint sprig and lemon slice.

LIBATION NOTE

Mix it up seasonally by garnishing the julep with any manner of fruit. Think berries, kiwi, grapefruit peel, kumquat—whatever appeals.

Blanche Armagnac Sour

Blanche (white) Armagnac is unaged Armagnac that often exudes floral notes. A sibling to other typically unaged grape-based brandies like pisco or grappa, it has long existed but only won coveted Appellation d'Origine Contrôlée (AOC) status in 2005, with formal establishment of its geographic boundaries and production processes. Blanche Armagnac can be intimidating to those unfamiliar with it, but this elegant yet easy-drinking clear spirit makes aromatic cocktails along the lines of those of its fellow unaged brandies. For example, with its kinship to pisco in aroma and flavor, it makes a surprisingly beautiful variation of the Peruvian-born pisco sour. In this French-inspired cousin, the citrusy sour notes sing with the floral notes of the Armagnac (try Château de Laubade or another quality brand) and are softened by frothy egg white.

2 oz (60 ml) blanche Armagnac

½ oz (15 ml) fresh lime juice

½ oz (15 ml) simple syrup (1:1)

1 egg white

3–5 dots Angostura bitters for garnish

Makes 1 cocktail

COUPE GLASS

Combine the Armagnac, lime juice, simple syrup, and egg white in a shaker and dry-shake for about 30 seconds to emulsify and aerate the mixture. Add ice and shake vigorously until well chilled and frothy, 30–60 seconds. Strain into a coupe glass and garnish artfully with the Angostura bitters, leaving the dots as is or drawing a pick through them to create an attractive pattern.

Bonjour!

Sylvie's French 75

The French 75 is one of the world's most beloved libations for its stiff gin-laced hit in an otherwise elegant Champagne cocktail. Sylvie Grateau is French through and through, and her version just might amp up the French attitude with a rinse of pastis or absinthe. The cocktail dates to the early days of World War I, with some lore suggesting it was named after the powerful 75mm French artillery field gun that packed an extra punch. Others claim it was named after 75mm cannons by American and French allied fighter pilots who would toast the French 75 cannon with Cognac and Champagne when celebrating successful air raids. Although a Cognac riff on the French 75 appeared in print in the late 1940s (see the Champère Champagne Julep (page 70) for a Champagne-and-brandy cocktail), gin is the widely recognized base of the French 75.

¼ oz (7.5 ml) pastis or absinthe for rinsing

1½ oz (45 ml) gin

¾ oz (20 ml) fresh lemon juice

½ oz (15 ml) simple syrup (1:1)

3 dashes orange bitters

2 oz (60 ml) Champagne or dry sparkling wine, chilled

Lemon wedge for garnish

Makes 1 cocktail

CHAMPAGNE FLUTE OR COUPE GLASS

Rinse a champagne flute or coupe glass with the pastis and pour out the excess. Combine the gin, lemon juice, simple syrup, and bitters in a shaker. Add ice and shake vigorously until well chilled, 20–30 seconds. Strain into the prepared glass and top with the Champagne. Garnish with the lemon wedge.

Kir Royale

The Kir Royale, a sophisticated low-proof drink ideal for brunch or the aperitif hour, is named after Félix Kir, a Catholic curate who was elected the mayor of Dijon, France, at the end of World War II. Kir, a hero of the French Resistance who served as mayor of the city for nearly two decades, regularly served the original Kir and its Champagne variation, the Kir Royale, at official receptions, popularizing them far beyond the Burgundy region. For Emily and friends, the easy duo of sparkling wine and tart-sweet currant liqueur is a quintessential French café option—as light and doable during the day as it is predinner.

2 barspoons crème de cassis

5 oz (150 ml) Champagne or dry sparkling wine, chilled

Lemon twist for garnish

Makes 1 cocktail

CHAMPAGNE FLUTE

Pour the cassis into a chilled champagne flute and top with the Champagne. Garnish with the lemon twist.

Le Forum

This simple variation on a classic gin martini dates to 1920s Paris and the Le Forum bar, which closed in 2015 after nearly a century as Paris's second-oldest cocktail bar. It was also the longest-running family-owned bar for three generations of the Biolatto family (Joseph Biolatto went on to open the city's lauded Louisiana-themed bar, Baton Rouge, which sadly closed in 2019). Created by Le Forum founder Antoine Biolatto in 1929, the signature cocktail of a martini base with orange notes courtesy of Grand Marnier is straightforward but refined.

1½ fl oz (45 ml) gin

2 barspoons (5 ml) French dry vermouth (Le Forum typically used Noilly Prat extra dry)

4–5 drops Grand Marnier

Orange peel for garnish

Makes 1 cocktail

NICK AND NORA OR COCKTAIL GLASS

Combine the gin, vermouth, and Grand Marnier in a mixing glass filled with ice and stir until well chilled, 20–30 seconds. Strain into a chilled Nick and Nora or cocktail glass. Garnish with the orange peel.

"I like Paris, but I'm not really sure Paris likes me."

—EMILY

Sancerre Sangria

Mindy Chen says Sancerre is a breakfast wine. It can be an ideal brunch beverage, especially when it forms the base of a white sangria loaded with fresh fruit. Sancerre is a French wine appellation in the Loire Valley primarily known for its dry, crisp whites made from 100 percent Sauvignon Blanc grapes. You can also use another dry Sauvignon Blanc. Widely appreciated for its citrus, herbaceous, elderflower, and grassy notes, Sancerre wine is a happy partner to elderflower liqueur, floral fruits, tart citrus, and herbs, all of which turn up in this easy-to-sip sangria that, yes, works for breakfast.

1 bottle (750 ml) Sancerre or other dry Sauvignon Blanc

1½ cups (360 ml) St-Germain or other elderflower liqueur

¼ cup (60 ml) fresh orange juice

2 white peaches, halved, pitted, and cut into slivers

2 lemons, cut into thin wheels

6–8 fresh thyme sprigs for garnish

Makes about 6 drinks

STEMLESS WINEGLASS
OR ROCKS GLASS

Combine the Sancerre, St-Germain, orange juice, peaches, and lemons in a pitcher. Give the mixture a stir, then let sit for a bit to meld the flavors or refrigerate for up to overnight. Serve over ice in stemless wineglasses or rocks glasses. Garnish each glass with a thyme sprig.

Chicago Paris Fizz

Emily moved from her Chicago home to France, leaving behind her boyfriend and family for new adventures in Paris. Here, in tribute to Emily's Windy City roots, is a twist on a classic: the often forgotten rum-based Chicago fizz. Its origins are murky, but it was already being made before Prohibition at New York's Waldorf-Astoria, where it was known as a Chicago import. This fizzy, frothy delight is traditionally made with ruby port (or sometimes tawny port) from Portugal, which brings a lush red-wine vibe (with nutty undertones if you use tawny port). In this version, the Chicago fizz is married with a little French goodness, subbing out the port for a Merlot-forward red wine from France's Bordeaux region that keeps the drink's rosy-red color.

1 oz (30 ml) dark rum

1 oz (30 ml) Merlot or Bordeaux-blend red wine

½ oz (15 ml) fresh lemon juice

½ teaspoon superfine sugar

1 egg white

1–3 oz (30–90 ml) club soda

Makes 1 cocktail

STEMLESS WINE GLASS, COLLINS, OR HIGHBALL GLASS

Combine the rum, wine, lemon juice, sugar, and egg white in a shaker and dry-shake for 30–60 seconds to emulsify and aerate the mixture. Add ice and shake vigorously until well chilled and egg white is frothy, 40–60 seconds. Strain into a chilled collins or highball glass. Slowly top with the desired amount of club soda until the frothy layer rises to the top half of the glass.

Parisian

A classic cocktail of the 1920s, the Parisian appeared in *The Savoy Cocktail Book* by Harry Craddock of London's Savoy Hotel, published in 1930. Nearly a decade earlier, it had been included in *Harry's ABC of Mixing Cocktails* by Harry MacElhone, who moved in 1923 from London to Paris, where he bought the popular New York Bar. Both recipes call for equal parts of gin, vermouth, and crème de cassis, while other versions allow the vermouth to take center stage. In this vermouth-forward version, quality vermouth makes all the difference (try La Quintinye Vermouth Royal), keeping the drink dry, floral, and lush with black currant tartness.

1½ oz (45 ml) French dry vermouth

1 oz (30 ml) gin

½ oz (15 ml) crème de cassis

Blackberries and/or lemon twist for garnish

Makes 1 cocktail

COUPE GLASS

Combine the vermouth, gin, and crème de cassis in a mixing glass filled with ice and stir until well chilled, 20–30 seconds. Strain into a chilled coupe glass and garnish with the blackberries and/or lemon twist.

French Herbal & Bitter Liqueurs

CHARTREUSE

GÉNÉPY

SUZE

SALERS

Chartreuse Swizzle

One of the original cities that gave us bars and cocktails as we know them in the 1800s, San Francisco was also one of two pioneering bar cities (along with New York City) in the cocktail renaissance of recent decades, already reviving classics and pushing into new territory ahead of the rest of the world with culinary cocktails and the like in the 1990s. Marcovaldo Dionysos came out of this era in SF, creating the Chartreuse Swizzle in 2003 for a drink competition, which he won. Five years later, Dionysos was the opening bar manager for chef Michael Mina's Clock Bar in San Francisco, where the drink became so popular that it was served at Mina restaurants across the country—and then quickly spread around the world. Featuring the legendary French spirit Chartreuse, made since the 1700s in the French Alps by Cartusian monks, this swizzle—a smart blend of tart lime, tropical pineapple, the almond and clove notes of Falernum, and herbaceous green Chartreuse—is ideal for modern-day Paris.

1½ oz (45 ml) green Chartreuse

1 oz (30 ml) pineapple juice

¾ oz (20 ml) fresh lime juice

½ oz (15 ml) Falernum

Fresh mint sprig and pineapple wedge for garnish

Makes 1 cocktail

COLLINS GLASS

Combine the Chartreuse, pineapple juice, lime juice, and Falernum in a collins glass and fill the glass with crushed ice. Swizzle the drink with a barspoon until the glass appears frosty. Top with more crushed ice, then garnish with the mint sprig and pineapple wedge.

Last Word

First mixed at the Detroit Athletic Club around 1915, this pre-Prohibition cocktail of green Chartreuse, gin, maraschino liqueur, and lime juice has seen multiple revivals over the decades. It reappeared in the 1951 book *Ted Saucier's Bottoms Up*, then was forgotten again until bartender Murray Stenson began serving it at Seattle's Zig Zag Café in the early aughts, when it was also showing up in bars around San Francisco. Ever since, it has been a cocktail geek's favorite the world over and continues to "trend" again every few years at notable cocktail bars. Its impeccable balance and layered flavors make it a truly great drink from aperitif hour into late night.

¾ oz (20 ml) gin

¾ oz (20 ml) green Chartreuse

¾ oz (20 ml) maraschino liqueur

¾ oz (20 ml) fresh lime juice

Lime wheel for garnish

Makes 1 cocktail

COUPE GLASS

Combine the gin, Chartreuse, maraschino liqueur, and lime juice in a shaker. Add ice and shake vigorously until well chilled, 20–30 seconds. Strain into a chilled coupe glass. Garnish with the lime wheel.

LIBATION NOTE

Maraschino liqueur, popularized by the Luxardo family since the nineteenth century, is unrelated to the neon-red cherries of the same name long popular in the United States. Instead of injecting a cloying sweetness into the Last Word, the liqueur releases a complex mix of herbal, nutty, and sweet layers.

Yellow Cocktail

Franck Audoux's charming Cravan bar in the 16th arrondissement is housed in a pocket-size Art Nouveau space that feels like time-traveling to 1920s Paris. For this sunny-hued cocktail, a layered beauty inspired by a drink popular on the French Riviera a century ago, Audoux plays with bitter, sour, and herbaceous notes to create a modern-day classic with southern French roots—a cocktail Emily would have surely enjoyed on her visit to the French Riviera in Season 2.

¾ oz (20 ml) London dry gin

¾ oz (20 ml) gentian liqueur, such as Suze or Salers

¾ oz (20 ml) yellow Chartreuse

¾ oz (20 ml) fresh lemon juice

Lemon twist for garnish

Makes 1 cocktail

COUPE GLASS

Combine the gin, gentian liqueur, Chartreuse, and lemon juice in a shaker. Add ice and shake vigorously until well chilled, 20–30 seconds. Strain into a chilled coupe glass. Garnish with the lemon twist.

Suze and Tonic

First produced in the late nineteenth century, Suze is made from gentian root, which grows in the Swiss and French Alps, along with a bouquet of undisclosed aromatics. It's a vibrant yellow, pleasingly bitter spirit in the family of French gentian liqueurs that includes Salers and Avèze. It can be paired with tonic for a low-ABV alternative to a gin and tonic—easy to make and a gratifying summer refresher. If you like, elevate it with an orange slice or even a couple of drops of Angostura bitters. But the straight-up two-ingredient original is utterly pleasing on its own.

1½ oz (45 ml) Suze

Tonic water to taste

Lemon twist for garnish

Makes 1 cocktail

COLLINS GLASS

Fill a collins glass with ice. Add the Suze, then top with the tonic water. Garnish with the lemon twist.

Old Pal

In some ways, it's surprising that the Boulevardier, a classic variation on the great Negroni that replaces the gin with bourbon whiskey, took off globally over the Old Pal, a drier, less sweet Negroni variation. In the 1920s, Scottish-born Harry MacElhone of Paris's famed Harry's New York Bar created a recipe for the Old Pal, which swaps out the gin for rye whiskey and the sweet vermouth for dry vermouth. The Old Pal drinks lighter and drier than the Boulevardier while packing the same bitter punch.

1 oz (30 ml) rye whiskey
1 oz (30 ml) Campari
1 oz (30 ml) dry vermouth
Blood orange slice for garnish

Makes 1 cocktail
ROCKS GLASS

Combine the whiskey, Campari, and vermouth in a mixing glass filled with ice and stir until well chilled, 20–30 seconds. Strain into a rocks glass over ice. Garnish with the orange slice.

French White Negroni

British bartender Wayne Collins created the White Negroni in 2001 at Vinexpo, a major beverage trade show in Bordeaux. His Negroni riff went French with bittersweet Suze, the legendary gentian-based liqueur, and wine-based Lillet Blanc. When Audrey Saunders soon after put Collins's inspired spin on her menu at the Pegu Club in New York City, it took off almost immediately and then went global. While the drink was originally made with equal parts of each ingredient (just like a classic Negroni), it's more common two decades later to see the gin upped and the Suze cut back. Of course, bitter hounds can go equal parts for a more bracing cocktail.

1½ oz (45 ml) gin

1 oz (30 ml) Lillet Blanc

½ oz (15 ml) Suze

Citrus slice for garnish

Makes 1 cocktail

ROCKS GLASS

Combine the gin, Lillet Blanc, and Suze in a mixing glass filled with ice and stir until well chilled, 20–30 seconds. Strain into a rocks glass over ice. Garnish with the citrus slice.

Génépy and Pear Tonic

Génépy is a style of alpine herbal liqueur from the Western Alps and is particularly historic in France and Italy. It is drunk as both an aperitif and a digestif. More gentle than Chartreuse and absinthe, génépy has a soft, herbaceous quality that adds intrigue to cocktails without a heavy hit of bitterness. It is especially refreshing and crushable with tonic, dry vermouth, and a splash of poire Williams (pear eau-de-vie).

1 oz (30 ml) génépy

1 oz (30 ml) dry vermouth

½ oz (15 ml) poire Wiliams

1–4 oz (30–120 ml) tonic water

Pear slice and fresh thyme or rosemary sprig

Makes 1 cocktail

COLLINS GLASS

Combine the génépy, vermouth, and poire Williams in a collins glass filled with ice and stir until well chilled, 20–30 seconds. Strain into a collins glass over ice and top with the tonic water. Garnish with the pear slice and thyme sprig to bring out the botanicals in the génépy and vermouth.

Bijou

The Bijou, which appears in the 1900 edition of Harry Johnson's *Bartenders' Manual*, is a favorite of cocktail geeks for its winning marriage of gin with the herbal complexity of Chartreuse and sweet vermouth. It was popular before Prohibition but was essentially forgotten until the 2000s, when some savvy barkeeps revived it. Originally calling for equal parts of the three ingredients plus orange bitters, a reduced amount of sweet vermouth and green Chartreuse allows for a more balanced drink—a robust beauty that is as chic as it is bold.

1½ oz (45 ml) gin

1 oz (30 ml) sweet vermouth

¾ oz (20 ml) green Chartreuse

2 dashes orange bitters

Luxardo maraschino cherry for garnish

Makes 1 cocktail

NICK AND NORA GLASS

Combine the gin, vermouth, Chartreuse, and bitters in a mixing glass filled with ice and stir until well chilled, 20–30 seconds. Strain into a chilled Nick and Nora glass. Garnish with the cherry.

"He never misses a Champagne toast. Especially when it's for him."

—SYLVIE

La Tour Eiffel

American cocktail pioneer and author Gary "Gaz" Regan sadly passed away in 2019. But he left behind an enduring legacy, including a highly influential cocktail-renaissance book, *The Joy of Mixology* (2003), and his Regan's Orange Bitters No. 6, now a staple of countless backbars.

Regan got the idea for La Tour Eiffel while touring distilleries in Cognac, France. He reimagined the original Sazerac, which was a Cognac cocktail with all-French elements: Cointreau, Suze, and absinthe. Orange notes shine along with the bittersweet accent of Suze, while a hint of absinthe adds anise intrigue. Suze launched in 1889, just as the Eiffel Tower opened, later inspiring Regan's naming of the cocktail. This cocktail has a smoother finish than Emily's dream about the Eiffel Tower.

2½ oz (75 ml) XO Cognac

½ oz (15 ml) Cointreau or orange curaçao

½ oz (15 ml) Suze

¼ oz (7.5 ml) absinthe

Lemon twist for garnish

Makes 1 cocktail

CHAMPAGNE FLUTE

Combine the Cognac, Cointreau, Suze, and absinthe in a mixing glass filled with ice and stir until well chilled, 20–30 seconds. Strain into a chilled champagne flute and garnish with the lemon twist.

LIBATION NOTE

If less absinthe is preferred, rinse the chilled champagne flute with ¼ oz (7.5 ml) absinthe and pour out the excess, then omit the absinthe in the mixing glass.

Camille's Refresher

Where Gabriel's heart is concerned, Camille can be territorial with Emily, but in all other ways, she's hospitable and generous, connecting Emily more deeply with Parisian life and French culture. Casual and refreshing, this tribute to Camille layers génépy and gin and subtly releases their botanical flavor profile with fresh cucumber and lime juices. The drink is French while also being universal, and is a cocktail that easily moves from day into night.

1½ oz (45 ml) gin

½ oz (15 ml) génépy

1 oz (30 ml) cucumber juice (page 123)

¾ oz (20 ml) fresh lime juice

½ oz (15 ml) simple syrup (1:1)

Pinch of sea salt

Thin cucumber strip for garnish

Makes 1 cocktail

ROCKS GLASS

Combine the gin, génépy, cucumber juice, lime juice, simple syrup, and salt in a shaker. Add ice and shake vigorously until well chilled, 20–30 seconds. Strain into a rocks glass over a large ice cube. Garnish with the cucumber strip.

French Mocktails

Lavender Citron Pressé

Citron pressé is a staple of French café life. Essentially a deconstructed lemonade—with lemon juice, water, and sweetener each served separately—it allows you to mix your drink to your desired sweet-tart balance. You can change up this recipe, using plain instead of lavender simple syrup, or you can make a rosemary syrup and garnish with rosemary.

5 lemons

1 cup (240 ml) lavender simple syrup (page 123)

Sparkling water, chilled, to taste

Makes 4 mocktails

COLLINS GLASS

Line up 4 collins glasses. Halve and squeeze the juice from 1 lemon, then strain through a fine-mesh sieve into a glass. Repeat with 3 more lemons and the remaining 3 glasses. Slice thin wheels from the remaining lemon and set them aside for garnish.

Add a spoonful of lavender simple syrup to a glass, stir together with the lemon juice, add ice, and top with sparkling water. Stir gently and taste, adding more syrup or additional lemon juice until you reach the desired sweet-tart balance. Fill the glass with more ice if needed. Repeat with the remaining glasses, then garnish each glass with a lemon wheel and a lavender bud.

Perrier Pineapple Punch

The iconic French mineral water brand, Perrier, has been a staple since 1863. On a hot summer—or warm spring or fall—day, this easy punch-like Perrier-and-pineapple mocktail is a breezy refresher.

Fresh herb leaves, such as rosemary, thyme, and sage, for the ice cubes

1½ oz (45 ml) pineapple juice

½ oz (15 ml) fresh lime juice

¼ oz (7.5 ml) simple syrup (1:1)

3–5 drops nonalcoholic aromatic bitters, such as All the Bitter brand

2–3 oz (60-90 ml) Perrier mineral water

Pineapple wedge and/or 1–2 fresh herb sprigs for garnish

Makes 1 mocktail

COLLINS GLASS

At least 1 day before making the mocktail, place the herb leaves, whole or trimmed to fit, in the molds of an empty ice-cube tray, add water to fill the mold one-third full, and place the tray in the freezer until the water freezes. Remove from the freezer, add more water to fill two-thirds full, and return to the freezer until frozen. (Adding the water in two steps will ensure the herbs are suspended in the cubes, as they will float to the top with the first addition of water.) Pop the cubes free of the tray, pack into a lock-stop plastic bag, and store in the freezer until needed.

Combine the pineapple juice, lime juice, simple syrup, and bitters in a shaker. Add ice and shake vigorously until well chilled, 20–30 seconds. Strain into a collins glass and fill with the herb ice. Top with the Perrier and garnish with the pineapple wedge and/or herb sprigs.

Zero-Proof French 75

A conceivable sipper for Emily at lunch during long workdays launching a new campaign—or for a lovely zero-proof alternative any time of day–this nonalcoholic version of the elegant French 75 (page 74) is a le choix parfait way to go. There are an ever-growing number of nonalcoholic (NA) spirits on the market, with NA gins like AMASS Riverine, Lyre's, GinIsh, and Cut Above, and NA sparkling wines like Prima Pavé, Lili, Fre, and St. Regis.

2 oz (60 ml) nonalcoholic gin

½ oz (15 ml) fresh lemon juice

½ oz (15 ml) simple syrup (1:1)

3 oz (90 ml) nonalcoholic sparkling wine

Lemon peel for garnish

Makes 1 mocktail

CHAMPAGNE FLUTE

Combine the gin, lemon juice, and simple syrup in a shaker. Add ice and shake vigorously until well chilled, 20–30 seconds. Strain into a chilled champagne flute. Top with sparkling wine. Garnish with the lemon peel.

"The French are romantics, but they're also realists."

—MINDY

Luc's Improved Ginger Beer

Wary of the new American in their office, Luc and Julien, Emily's new coworkers at Savoir, initally mock her, Luc with his signature dry humor. But not long after, Luc befriends Emily and helps her navigate the cultural differences. This gently spiced, fresh take on ginger beer celebrates Luc's easygoing but slightly spicy vibe. Straightforward yet flavor-packed, it is ideal for sipping on its own or for adding to a range of mocktails—or for mixing with your favorite spirit for a cocktail.

FOR THE GINGER SYRUP

1 cup (200 g) sugar

½ cup (120 ml) water

3 oz (90 g) fresh ginger (roughly the size of a large finger), peeled and chopped

2 pinches of sea salt

FOR THE GINGER BEER

6½ cups (1.5 l) club soda, chilled

½ cup (120 ml) fresh lime juice

6–8 lime wheels for garnish

Makes 4 pints (2 l); serves 6–8

COLLINS GLASS

To make the ginger syrup, in a small saucepan over medium heat, combine the sugar and water and heat, stirring, until the sugar dissolves. Reduce the heat to low, stir in the ginger and salt, and simmer, stirring occasionally, until the ginger softens, 2–5 minutes. Remove from the heat, cover, and let steep for 20–25 minutes. Strain the syrup through a fine-mesh sieve and discard the solids. The syrup can be made up to 2 weeks in advance. Store in a tightly capped glass jar in the refrigerator.

To make the beer, combine the club soda, lime juice, and ginger syrup in a pitcher and stir to mix well. Serve in collins glasses over ice. Garnish each glass with a lime wheel.

Strawberry Elderflower Fizz

This strawberry-infused mocktail evokes spring and summer and is an easy-drinking choice for brunch, for lunch, or with modest bites at aperitif time. A touch of cool cucumber marries well with the brightness of the berries and the flowery, subtly sweet elderflower syrup.

3 strawberries, hulled and sliced

1 oz (30 ml) elderflower syrup

2 oz (60 ml) fresh lime juice

1 oz (30 ml) plain water

1–3 oz (30–90 ml) tonic water

Cucumber wedge for garnish

Makes 1 mocktail

ROCKS GLASS

Muddle the strawberries in a shaker, then pour in the elderflower syrup, lime juice, and plain water. Add ice and shake vigorously until well chilled, 20–30 seconds. Double-strain into a rocks glass filled with ice. Top with the tonic water. Garnish with the cucumber wedge.

LIBATION NOTE

If you prefer a more vegetal mix of cucumber and strawberry, add a few cucumber slices to the shaker with the strawberries and muddle together.

Gentiana Spritz

In 2021, US-based craft mixer brand Top Note described Gentiana, its gentian-flavored tonic water, as "the first aperitivo soda in the United States featuring French gentian root in 145 years"—a US-French alliance that Emily can add with pride to this bright-tasting spritz. Gentiana delivers a bitter, citrusy punch like a lighter soda version of Suze, Campari, or your favorite amaro. It also works in an alcohol-free Negroni and other spritzes.

3 oz (90 ml) Gentiana

2 oz (60 ml) fresh orange juice

1 oz (30 ml) club soda or tonic water

1 dash nonalcoholic aromatic bitters, such as All the Bitter brand

Orange wheel for garnish

Makes 1 mocktail

WINEGLASS

Combine the Gentiana, orange juice, club soda, and bitters in a mixing glass filled with ice and stir until well chilled, 20–30 seconds. Strain into a wineglass over ice. Garnish with the orange wheel.

LIBATION NOTE

If you cannot find Gentiana, use an Italian bitter soda, such as Lurisia chinotto or ruby-red San Pellegrino Sanbittèr.

Julien's Faux-Proof Piña Colada

Julien keeps Emily up on the juiciest gossip in the offices of Savoir, which makes this piña colada that lacks alcoholic bite the ideal tribute to her fashionable coworker. It's like the best tropical, poolside, or beach beverage, with a touch of apple cider vinegar and salt to balance the sweetness.

3 oz (90 ml) pineapple juice

2½ oz (75 ml) cream of coconut, such as Coco López brand

¼ oz (7.5 ml) apple cider vinegar

¼ oz (7.5 ml) pure maple syrup

2 pinches of sea salt

Pineapple wedge, maraschino cherry, and freshly grated nutmeg for garnish

Makes 1 mocktail

HURRICANE GLASS

Combine the pineapple juice, cream of coconut, vinegar, maple syrup, salt, and ½ cup (120 ml) ice in a blender and blend until smooth. Pour into a hurricane glass. Garnish with the pineapple wedge, cherry, and a dusting of nutmeg.

Temperance Paloma

One of Mexico's most popular cocktails, the Paloma is traditionally made with tequila, but is also fabulous with mezcal. Its balance of tart lime and grapefruit benefits from a pinch of salt to brighten and tighten the flavors. This nonalcoholic version, which trades out the tequila for grapefruit soda, is as refreshing as the original, especially at brunch or the aperitif hour. Look for Jarritos, a popular Mexican grapefruit soda brand, or an artisanal grapefruit soda.

1½ oz (45 ml) fresh grapefruit juice

1 oz (30 ml) fresh lime juice

¼ oz (7.5 ml) simple syrup (1:1)

Pinch of sea salt

1 oz (30 ml) grapefruit soda

Grapefruit and lime wedges for garnish

Makes 1 mocktail

COLLINS OR HIGHBALL GLASS

Combine the grapefruit juice, lime juice, simple syrup, and salt in a shaker. Add ice and shake vigorously until well chilled, 15–20 seconds. Strain into a collins or highball glass over ice. Top with the grapefruit soda. Garnish with the grapefruit and lime wedges.

Cucumber Juice

2 large English cucumbers

½ cup (120 ml) water

Makes about 2 cups (475 ml)

Peel the cucumbers and halve lengthwise. Using the large holes of a box grater, grate the cucumber halves into a bowl. Transfer to a blender or food processor and add the water, using less if the grated flesh looks watery. Blend or process until smooth. Strain the mixture through a fine-mesh sieve lined with cheesecloth and discard the solids. The juice will keep in an airtight container in the refrigerator for up to 3 days.

Melon Juice

1 cup (160 g) cantaloupe or honeydew melon cubes

½ cup (120 ml) water

Makes about 1 cup (235 ml)

In a blender, combine the melon and water and blend at high speed until the melon is completely puréed, about 30 seconds. Strain the mixture through a fine-mesh sieve lined with cheesecloth and discard the solids. The juice will keep in an airtight container in the refrigerator for up to 3 days.

Lavender Simple Syrup

1 cup (240 ml) water

1 cup (200 g) sugar

2 teaspoons dried culinary lavender buds

Makes about 1½ cups (350 ml)

In a small saucepan over medium heat, combine the water and sugar and bring to a simmer, stirring until the sugar dissolves. Let simmer 2–3 minutes, then remove from the heat, add the lavender buds, and let steep until cool. Strain the syrup through a fine-mesh sieve into a glass jar and discard the lavender buds. Cap tightly and refrigerate for up to 2 weeks.

Index

weldon**owen**

PO Box 3088
San Rafael, CA 94912
www.weldonowen.com

WELDON OWEN INTERNATIONAL
CEO Raoul Goff
Publisher Roger Shaw
Associate Publisher Amy Marr
Editorial Director Katie Killebrew
Assistant Editor Kayla Belser
VP Creative Chrissy Kwasnik
Art Director Allister Fein
VP Manufacturing Alix Nicholaeff
Sr Production Manager Joshua Smith
Sr Production Manager, Subsidiary Rights
Lina s Palma-Temena

Photography Waterbury Publications,
Des Moines, IA
Food Stylist Jennifer Peterson

A WELDON OWEN PRODUCTION

Printed and bound in China

All rights reserved. No part of this book
may be reproduced in any form without
written permission from the publisher.

First printed in 2023
10 9 8 7 6 5 4 3 2 1

Library of Congress Cataloging in
Publication data is available

ISBN: 979-8-88674-023-3

Weldon Owen would also like to thank
Rachel Markowitz and Sharon Silva.